CONTENTS

PREFACE

A few years ago I started noticing mission statements in the businesses I frequented—at the car rental, the pharmacy, even a funeral home. At the YMCA, I swim surrounded by the Y's tagline—"We build strong kids, strong families, strong communities"—and by its core values: "Caring, Honesty, Respect, Responsibility." I also enjoy seeing the Chicago Public Library's branding statement, "Read, Learn, Discover," based on its mission, turn up in new places.

One of my favorite mission statements appears in red capital letters at a take-out restaurant called Hecky's Barbecue. Titled "What We're About," it reads:

> "Giving our customers the best B.B.Q. anywhere!
> Doing it with fun, flair, excellence and excitement!
> Serving our customers quickly, courteously and with camaraderie!
> We appreciate your comments and suggestions."

Another appears in "The Motley Fool," a syndicated column that appears in newspapers across the country. It reads:

> "Our mission: to inform, to amuse and to help you make money."

Each of these mission statements makes a powerful and unique statement about the purpose and passion of its creators. What does your mission statement say about you? Is it the image you want to project? Do you use it to promote your library?

Seeing mission statements colorfully written and prominently posted opened my eyes to their power. I began to wonder why more libraries don't make better use of their mission statements.

Having worked twenty-plus years in library marketing and communication, I've observed that much of what libraries communicate is unconscious. Most libraries don't have a communication plan. Librarians complain that their work is undervalued, but they are better at describing what they do—collect, organize, preserve, etc.—than at communicating why their work is important and the difference it makes in people's lives. All of the library directors interviewed for this book consider the mission statement an essential planning document, but few of them use it for promotional purposes. And although they feel confident that their staff members understand the intent, few directors believe their staff or board members could actually say their mission statements.

My mission in writing this handbook is to provide practical guidance and inspiration for writing a good mission statement, one that that works as both a planning and a communication tool. The focus is on libraries, but the advice given applies to any organization that is driven by service rather than profit. Chapter 5 of the book presents sample mission and vision statements from a cross section of libraries, library foundations, Friends, and other organizations.

My thanks go to Peggy Barber, my business partner, friend, and mentor, for sharing her insight and support; to the many institutions that granted permission to reprint their mission statements; and to those who patiently and thoroughly answered my questions.

As a former journalist and public relations person, I place great value on words. I believe a mission statement can and should be a powerful tool. But writing is the easy part. This book is dedicated to all of the librarians and library staff who bring their libraries' missions to life.

CHAPTER 1

Putting the Mission in a Mission Statement

Imagine walking into a party or job interview and someone asks about the library. You reply: "Our library is a learning center where a wide range of materials, resources, necessary equipment, and services are accessible to both students and teachers. The media center supports, complements, and expands the work of the classroom and curriculum with the goal of . . ."

Or: "Our library provides access and promotes the use of materials that serve the informational, recreational, educational, and cultural needs of the community. Access to information and ideas will be assured through an efficient and effective staff working in adequate facilities, commensurate with sound and responsible fiscal planning."

Or: "Our library provides information, services, and facilities adequate to support the instructional and research programs of the University, including the distance-learning component, and to stimulate a continuing interest on the part of the student in self-education and service . . ."

Or: "The mission of our Archives is to collect, preserve, and make available the records of the university. It assists departments in identifying records of enduring historical value and ensuring that those records are transferred to . . ."

Imagine your frustration as you watch the other person's interest fade to boredom. Unfortunately, that is the effect many library mission statements have, even on their own staffs. Instead of sparking interest, they kill it. They are hard to read, and even harder to say. What should be a conversation starter turns into a conversation stopper.

Consider some alternative responses:

> "We help people achieve their full potential." (Denver Public Library)

> "We bring together knowledgeable staff, scholarly information, welcoming spaces, and leading-edge technology to promote learning and enable research." (University of Texas-Arlington Libraries)

> "Our mission is to ensure that students and staff are effective users of ideas and information." (Traverse City Central High School Library Media Center)[1]

> "Our mission is to serve as the official memory of the University." (Ohio State University Archives)

All of the above responses are based on real library mission statements. The difference in tone and content speaks for itself: long and tedious versus short and punchy, process focused versus outcome focused.

Such brevity is the exception rather than the rule among mission statements of all types of libraries. Many are so ponderous that even staff and board members find them boring, which perhaps explains why so many library mission statements are nowhere to be seen or heard, at least in public.

Many librarians are surprised to learn that marketing communication is not about inventing something new and sexy to sell the library. It's about mission—and making a conscious effort to build understanding and appreciation for the library's role. Specific promotions that focus on services the library offers—on-line reference, preschool story hours, and other activities—need to happen in the context of an overall plan to position the library as an essential and valued resource.

There are many excellent books and articles that discuss strategic planning and the role of the mission statement in depth.[2] The premise of this book is that a well-written mission statement should both guide your library's planning and drive its marketing effort. It should deliver a message both to the library's "family"—its staff, board, and volunteers—and to its external audiences, which include users, institutional administrators, legislators, funders and potential funders, community leaders, and others the library wishes to influence and impress.

The evidence suggests that libraries of all types make little use of their mission statements in communicating what they are about. Of the hundreds of library websites that were searched for this book, fewer than half have their mission statements posted or posted in a way that is clearly identified, visible, or easily located. Only a handful display them on their home page. While academic and research libraries are most likely to post their mission statements, they generally do not post them on the home page. Public and school libraries are more likely to post them on their home page, but most don't post them at all in this most public of venues.

Despite evidence linking a well-written mission statement with high performance, many businesses don't do much better.[3] This is changing, especially among smaller—some might say smarter—firms. Southwest Airlines is one that posts its mission on its website:

> "The mission of Southwest Airlines is dedication to the highest quality of Customer Service delivered with a sense of warmth, friendliness, individual pride, and Company Spirit."

The Vermont Country Store says its mission is

> "To sell merchandise that doesn't come back—to people who do."

Mollie Stone's, a West Coast grocery chain, posts its mission statement at the entrance of its stores and on the back of employee business cards:

> "Our mission is to surpass customer expectations with superior customer service, exciting variety, and quality of products in a fun and positive environment for our customers and employees."

For nonprofit organizations, a potent mission statement is essential to attracting financial and volunteer support. In its book *Profiles of Excellence*, Independent Sector, a national coalition dedicated to strengthening philanthropy and nonprofit initiatives, cites a clear and focused mission statement as the primary characteristic of successful nonprofit organizations.[4]

The United Way of America has as its mission:

> "To improve people's lives by mobilizing the caring power of communities."

The mission of Big Brothers Big Sisters, an organization that pairs children with adult mentors, is

> "To develop quality mentoring relationships inspiring youth to be confident, competent, and caring individuals in our community."

The YMCA's mission appears on its home page and throughout its website:

> "To put Christian principles into practice through programs that build healthy spirit, mind, and body for all."

The Y's tagline, or branding statement, which appears on all promotional materials, is a variation of its mission statement: "We build strong kids, strong families, strong communities."

To be effective as a planning tool, planning experts tell us that a mission statement should

- Establish focus.
- Identify who is served and how.
- Motivate staff and donors.
- Provide a measure of effectiveness.[5]

To be effective as a communication tool, your mission statement should also pack a punch. It should deliver a clear, brief, and dynamic message. And it should be easily said as well as read.

The three preceding statements work as both planning and communication tools. They are focused, clear, and measurable. They identify who is served and how the mission is carried out. They also convey a commitment and caring that characterize their organization's public image.

Mission—not just what you do, but how you contribute and why you do it—is the quintessential part of any organization's identity. Goals, objectives, and activities or strategies all flow from mission. Having a statement that also works as a communication tool helps to ensure that your library will both *do* what it says and *say* what it does.

Notes

1. See appendix A, Model Mission Statement, American Association of School Librarians.
2. See Suggested Reading, page 77.
3. Patricia Jones and Larry Kahaner, *Say It and Live It: The 50 Corporate Mission Statements That Hit the Mark* (New York: Currency/Doubleday, 1995), ix–xii. Christopher K. Bart, "Mission Matters," *CPA Journal* 68, no.8 (1998): 56–57.
4. E. B. Knauft, Renee A. Berger, and Sandra T. Gray, *Profiles of Excellence: Achieving Success in the Nonprofit Sector.* A Publication of Independent Sector (San Francisco: Jossey-Bass, 1991), 3–8. Also see Richard Steckel and Jennifer Lehman, *In Search of America's Best Nonprofits* (San Francisco: Jossey Bass, 1997), 17.
5. See, for example, Smith, Bucklin & Associates, Inc., Robert H. Wilbur, ed., *The Complete Guide to Nonprofit Management,* 2d ed. (New York: Wiley, 2000); Sharon M. Oster, *Strategic Management for Nonprofit Organizations: Theory and Cases* (Oxford and New York: University Press, 1995).

CHAPTER 2

Marketing, Mission, and Message

Marketing is that function of the organization that can keep in constant touch with the organization's consumers, read their needs, develop products that meet these needs, and build a program of communications to express the organization's purposes.

—Philip Kotler and Sidney Levy[1]

If libraries are to be valued institutions, they must find ways to distinguish themselves from their competition, which is what marketing is designed to do. A mission statement that sends a clear message about the library's unique role and contribution is an essential first step.

There are five key elements in a strategic marketing plan:

1. *Research*—To determine target audiences, the needs and wants of consumers, and levels of customer satisfaction and to collect other relevant data.
2. *Planning*—To develop services and delivery methods.
3. *Strategies*—To implement effective methods for providing service.
4. *Communication*—To build awareness and convey the value of what is offered.
5. *Evaluation*—To monitor effectiveness.

Many library administrators have been slow to adopt a marketing mind-set, which says that communicating about what you do is as important as doing it. This is changing in the face of superbookstores, the Internet, school, sports, and other activities that fill similar needs and compete for the public's time and attention.

The Planning for Results planning model endorsed by the Public Library Association (PLA) is essentially a market-driven approach, with the library's mission statement, goals, objectives, and activities stemming from an assessment of community needs and of library programs and services.[2]

But while most libraries have a service plan, few have a communication plan. Very few employ communication professionals. In many cases, library communication is a responsibility shared among several staff who—in the absence of any clearly defined, overall strategy—exercise their best judgment and creativity. This scatter-shot approach violates basic advertising principles and common sense, which tell us the more a message is used, the more likely it is to be remembered.

A communication plan is an essential part of marketing because it provides a map for projecting a clear and distinctive image.[3] It identifies target audiences and strategies for reaching them. At its core is the key message.

A key message is a simple, clear, and compelling statement that focuses on the most important thing you want people to know about the library—what marketers refer to as its unique selling proposition. With a bit of editing and creativity, the library's mission statement can and should serve as its key message. It should provide a foundation for all its communications, including promotional materials, website, and presentations to community groups.[4]

A mission statement that also serves as a key message helps to ensure consistency in how the library defines and presents itself. It should drive the library's marketing effort both in developing services and in communicating about them.

The questions posed in figure 2-1 will help you assess the strengths and weaknesses of your library's mission statement.

WHAT MAKES A GOOD MISSION STATEMENT?

A good mission statement shouldn't be boring, especially to you and your staff. What you say should be what you deliver, and it should be said in a way that commands attention and inspires enthusiasm.

Like most good writing, your mission statement should be simple and direct. It should avoid the pompous and trite. To be most effective, it should be

FIGURE 2-1
What Does Your Mission Statement Say about Your Library?

In evaluating your library's mission statement, ask the following questions:

- Does it communicate the most important thing you want people to know and remember?
- Does it convey the unique benefits offered by the library?
- Does it inspire enthusiasm among employees, partners, and funders?
- Is it simple and memorable? Would it pass the T-shirt test?
- Are the language and content current?
- Does the tone complement the image you wish for your library? For example, if one of your goals is to provide a welcoming atmosphere, does your mission statement sound inviting?

realistic, compelling, and sincere: realistic if it is to be achievable, compelling if it is to have impact, and sincere if it is to be credible.

In his book *Straight to the Heart,* Barry Feig makes the case that marketing success starts with the heart and that a "concise, consumer-driven mission statement is a stepping stone to winning the hearts and minds of customers."[5] Feig's case is one that most of us understand. We consumers make decisions based not just on logic, but on how we feel. What we really want to know is not how a product or service works but how it will make a difference in our lives. That is what makes a message compelling. We visit dentists not to have our teeth cleaned, but so we will have healthier, prettier teeth that will last longer. Much the same can be said for libraries. People don't just go to their school, public, or academic libraries to borrow materials or do research. They are there to learn, enjoy, and let their minds and spirits soar.

In short, mission statements shouldn't be literal statements of what the library does. They should focus on the distinctive contribution of the library and the outcomes or benefits it offers. A good mission statement is one that makes us feel our corner of the world is a better place because of the library. And it makes everyone connected with it feel proud.

Some examples:

"The Denton Public Library enriches and advances the community by providing quality materials and services of informational, educational, leisure, and cultural value."

"The mission of the Bethel College Library is to create a stimulating environment, which will promote the quest of knowledge and encourage academic excellence."

"The mission of the McCrorey-Liston Elementary Library Media Center is to ensure that every child has the opportunity to explore his world through a variety of books and resources. We strive to help all students become independent users of information and lifelong readers."

Simple and straightforward, the above statements communicate exactly what these libraries are about. The focus is on the library's contribution, not on the process. Originally conceived as a planning tool, mission statements in the past tended to be longer and more cumbersome. They were strong on content but often lacked style. Planning experts agree that in today's world, shorter is better. A simple, well-crafted mission statement is less likely to be filed away and more likely to succeed for both planning and communication purposes.

Most of the mission statements in this book were adopted in the last decade, when shorter mission statements became the norm. But mission statements are getting even shorter. Instead of two or three sentences, most experts recommend one. Management guru Peter Drucker says the mission statement should fit on a T-shirt.[6] Another expert says it should be understood by a twelve-year-old.[7] Few libraries have been bold enough to take the T-shirt approach. Three that have are the Daly City Public Library in California, the Orange County Public Library in Florida, and the Lawrence High School Library in Kansas.

The Daly City Public Library's mission statement reads:

"Preserving yesterday
Informing today
Inspiring tomorrow"

The Orange County Library System statement:

"Information, Imagination, Inspiration"

The Lawrence High School statement:

"Lawrence High School
Resources
Education
Adventure
Diversity
Success
At the Library!"

At the suggestion of Marilyn Hoffman, head of the community relations department, the Orange County Library Board adopted its mission statement in 2002 after a series of visioning sessions with the public, staff, board, and library managers. The phrase had previously been used as a tagline on library promotional materials. "I suggested that this could be our mission statement because it shows action, is short and easy to remember, and embodies all that we do now and hope to do in the future," explains Hoffman.

The Chicago Public Library has digested its mission statement into three words:

"Read, Learn, Discover!"[8]

The shorter, slogan-type mission statement is still the exception rather than the rule. But you will find many examples of mission statements in this book that could be adapted for T-shirts. This is not to say that all mission statements should sound like slogans or what is sometimes called a branding statement, the ultimate distillation of identity.[9] But it should be memorable, meaningful, and easily adapted for different formats, including a branding statement.

WHAT MAKES A BAD MISSION STATEMENT?

Everyone knows what libraries and librarians do, right? They acquire and organize books, CDs, videos, and other materials. They check out books. They answer questions. They assist researchers. They plan programs. They preserve our cultural heritage. They teach students to be information literate.

Yawn. Librarians do their best to provide something for everyone, or at least for their clients. But too many brochures and websites rely on itemized listings of services to tell the library's story. A succinct statement of the library's unique contribution is seldom to be found. And the reaction by even a motivated reader is that there is simply too much information.

Most bad mission statements sound like they were written by a committee, and they probably were. Instead of sounding noble, they sound like to-do lists. A truly bad mission statement fails as both a planning tool and a communication tool. It doesn't provide a clear and measurable statement of intent. And it doesn't communicate why the organization exists and the difference it makes. These failures generally stem from one of several misguided strategies.

The "mission as vision statement" approach confuses these two key elements of a strategic plan. The mission statement is present tense. It is a here-and-now statement of who we are, what we do, and why. The vision statement paints the long-range picture of where the library is going and what it wants to happen when it gets there (see figure 2-2). Many strategic plans also include a statement of philosophy, values, or guiding principles, such as diversity, intellectual freedom, and customer service. These are generally best kept separate from the mission statement.

The "kitchen sink" approach attempts to encompass all the various ways the library serves. The resulting list is impossible to remember, pleases no one, and means little to anyone. It also means that unless the library has unlimited resources it is doomed to fall short in some areas. If plans are to be more than good intentions, they must focus on what is most important, doable, and supportable. When it comes to powerful communication, less is generally more.

The "me too" approach is a tack frequently taken by school and academic libraries. It states: "The mission of the —— Library is to support the mission of the —— College/School." This pro forma approach begs the questions: What exactly does the library do? What is the value it brings? While it is a good idea to express support for the parent institution, the library's mission statement should first zero in on its own role.

The "more is better" approach takes three sentences to say what could be said in one; four-syllable words to say what could be said in two. Tedious to read, it is impossible to remember and say. Instead of being a source of inspiration, it is left to rest in peace by those who would like to think they understand what the mission statement means even if they can't repeat it.

The best way to avoid these pitfalls is to take time to write a statement that serves as both a planning and communication tool—one that is thoughtful, dynamic, and to the point.

FIGURE 2-2
Mission versus Vision

Compare and contrast these mission and vision statements.

Mission

"The mission of the Greenwich Library System is to provide free and convenient access to information and to promote a love of reading and research, the joy of lifelong learning and engagement with the arts, sciences and humanities."

Vision

"The constant vision of the Greenwich Library System is to provide the community with superior library services, to serve as the cultural and intellectual crossroads of Greenwich, and to be a leader among public libraries in a changing world."

Mission

"The South Carolina State Library's mission is to improve library services throughout the state and to ensure all citizens access to libraries and information resources adequate to meet their needs. The State Library supports libraries in meeting the informational, educational, cultural, and recreational needs of the people of South Carolina."

Vision

"The South Carolina State Library is a major leader in the planning and implementation of effective informational and library services for the people of South Carolina. It is a vital component of the State's information infrastructure."

Mission

"The University of Texas at Arlington Libraries bring together knowledgeable staff, scholarly information, welcoming spaces, and leading-edge technology to promote learning and enable research. First and foremost we serve UTA students and faculty. We also serve as a valuable resource for University staff and for the community beyond the campus."

Vision

"We will know we are succeeding when . . .
. . . the library is a center of academic life.
. . . our physical spaces promote research, reflection, collaboration.
. . . our virtual space offers resources and services anywhere, anytime.
. . . all resources and services are easy to use.
. . . all users are information fluent.
. . . our investment in staff, information resources, and technology promotes academic success and lifelong learning."

Mission

"The library media centers of the Beverly Public School System offer a wide variety of programs and services centered on reading and information literacy which:

> promote access to a variety of media, including print, nonprint, and electronic formats;
> provide instruction in the location, evaluation, and use of information;
> stimulate student interest in reading;
> support the curriculum of the schools."

Vision

"The vision of the library media centers of the Beverly Public Schools is to provide every student with a foundation for lifelong learning and ensure that students and staff are effective users of ideas and information."

Notes

1. Philip Kotler and Sidney Levy, "Broadening the Concept of Marketing," *Journal of Marketing* (January 1969).
2. Sandra Nelson for the Public Library Association, *The New Planning for Results: A Streamlined Approach* (Chicago: American Library Association, 2001).
3. See appendix B for a Communication Plan Worksheet.
4. For examples of key messages, see the American Library Association, "Campaign for America's Libraries." Available at www.ala.org/pio/. Accessed 11 April 2003.
5. Barry Feig, *Straight to the Heart* (New York: AMACOM, 1997).
6. Leader to Leader Institute (formerly the Drucker Foundation), "How to Develop a Mission Statement." 1999. Available at http://leadertoleader.org/leaderbooks/sat/mission.html/. Accessed 4 April 2003.
7. Laurie Beth Jones, *The Path: Creating Your Mission Statement for Work and Life* (New York: Hyperion, 1996).
8. See page 43 for the full text of the Chicago Public Library's mission statement.
9. For a discussion of branding and role of mission statements, see Patricia Tan, "Down to the Core: Branding Not-for-Profits." Available at http://www.brandchannel.com/features_effect.asp?id=140. Accessed 10 April 2003.

CHAPTER 3

Writing a
Mission Statement

Crafting a mission statement that works as both a planning and communication tool may take extra thought but will add greatly to its effectiveness. The biggest challenge in writing a mission statement is to communicate the distinct role and value of *your* library.

While all types of libraries share a universal mission of connecting their users with ideas and information, how a library fulfills this mission and toward what end—helping users prepare for a new career, assisting researchers, or nurturing a love of reading in children—will vary greatly.

Are your users primarily children, seniors, students, researchers, or all of the above? Does your library exist primarily to provide popular reading or as an educational or cultural resource? What does it do and why is this important? What sets it apart from other libraries, other departments, institutions, or services?

The answers should be clear from your library's mission statement. For example:

The Howard University Libraries in Washington, D.C., cite a

> "distinct commitment to preparing people of color and the economically disadvantaged for leadership and service to our nation and the global community."

Idaho State University points out that

"As the largest state-supported library in southeast Idaho, the
Libraries also play a role in the development of University
cooperative programs and in the provision of library services
to the citizens of Idaho."

The Timberwood Middle School Library Media Center in Humble, Texas,
points to its "broad collection of print and nonprint media."

The Camden Public Library in Maine describes itself as "a cultural and intellectual center for the community."

Unfortunately, many library mission statements fail to focus on a critical
aspect of what sets them apart—something bookstores don't offer and can't be
accessed on the Internet—the expert and personal assistance provided by librarians and other library staff. A good mission statement should spotlight the
human resources libraries offer as well as the material.

Remember that the tone of the statement will say as much as the words. The
language in your mission statement should be in keeping with the image you
wish to convey, whether that is formal or informal, lofty, or lively. Like most
good writing, your mission statement should be simple and direct. More and
bigger words don't necessarily convey more. Sometimes they just muddy the
message. The best statements are personal in tone and manage to say a lot in few
words.

The end result should inspire and motivate your staff—the people who
must live the mission if it is to have meaning—as well as others you wish to
impress and influence.

One of the world's great research libraries, the Library of Congress, says simply:

"The Library's mission is to make its resources available and
useful to the Congress and the American people and to sustain
and preserve a universal collection of knowledge and creativity
for future generations."

TIPS FOR WRITING MISSION STATEMENTS

• Aim for one—no more than three—short sentences. Saying more with less
  should be your goal.

• Avoid jargon that members of the public may not understand and buzzwords
  that quickly date.

• Ban bullet points. Bulleted points generally read better than they talk. If you
  must use them, limit them to three, which is all most people can remember.

- Use active voice. Writing in the active voice can make the difference between a statement that is pleasing and one that is powerful.
- Personalize the statement. Try using "our" rather than "the library's."
- Don't feel you have to start with the words "Our mission is . . ." Go directly to the point.
- Choose words that are meaningful to your audiences—all of them.
- Be specific about what you aim to accomplish. Again, limit yourself to three key points.
- Describe the most important thing your library does as though you were telling a friend.
- Write in a tone that is appropriate for your library, your parent institution, or community.
- Say the statement out loud to see whether it flows off the tongue. Try saying it the next day to see if you can remember it.
- Edit ruthlessly. Fewer adjectives and adverbs generally make for stronger sentences.
- Remember, it's only words—but words are powerful.

The importance of being current

Strategic plans used to be done for ten years, then five years, then three. Some joke now that a year is long range. Changing technology and changing times— socially, politically, and economically—demand constant monitoring and reassessment. If a library is to be perceived as dynamic and relevant, its mission statement must reflect these changes. For example, many mission statements used to include the phrase "in all formats." A few short years later, technology has become so widespread that the phrase seems dated and redundant. As information becomes more freely available electronically, many libraries are shifting their focus to the library as a community/educational/cultural center.

A library's mission statement should be reviewed and updated at least every three years. Many institutions review their mission statement as part of the annual planning process.

Words to avoid

Some words don't age well. Others look better than they sound. When in doubt, use simple, standard English that transcends time and political correctness.

Words and phrases like "world class," "stakeholders," and "exceed customer expectations" quickly become clichéd. Avoid words that smack of jargon—library, technical, and otherwise. While there may be times when no other word will do, use such words sparingly. Phrases like "in all formats" or "people of diverse backgrounds" are generally unnecessary. And qualifiers such as "adequate" can undermine your message.

A few examples and substitutes:

Access/Accessible—Libraries may provide access to the Internet, but they provide books, videos, and other services. The word "access" is generally unnecessary. Replace "accessible" with "available," or use the active voice (e.g., "The library provides . . .").

Collaborate—Cooperate, work with

Empower—Help, support

Enhance—Improve, expand

Facilitate—Help, assist

Database—On-line collection

Diverse—All, many, wide-ranging, varied, multicultural

Interloan—Borrow/loan from another library

Quality—Use this word with care; people will assume your mission is not to provide inferior service.

Utilize—Use

Figure 3-1 lists more than 150 verbs, nouns, and adjectives that would work well in a mission statement.

Writing it right

Keep in mind that a good mission statement should

- Be a source of guidance and inspiration.
- Define the unique contribution of your library.
- Be easy to say, read, and remember.

Process

Writing a mission statement is a good exercise in the democratic process . . . up to a point.

FIGURE 3-1

Words to Use

In addition to obvious words like *provide*, *support*, *information*, and *knowledge* try these:

Verbs

Achieve
Advance
Advise
Affirm
Assist
Build
Bridge
Connect
Cooperate
Consult
Create
Design
Develop
Discover
Educate
Encourage
Engage
Enable
Enliven
Enrich
Ensure
Expand
Explore
Extend
Foster
Grow
Help
Improve
Inspire
Inform
Lead
Learn
Link
Nourish
Nurture
Prepare

Promote
Pursue
Satisfy
Share
Stimulate
Strengthen
Teach
Uphold

Nouns

Adventure
Answers
Array
Attitudes
Awareness
Creativity
Community
Curiosity
Decision-making
Dreams
Education
Enjoyment
Excellence
Fun
Future
Hearts
Heritage
Home
Ideas
Interests
Inquiry
Imagination
Inspiration
Joy
Learning
Leadership
Life/lives

Love
Manage
Memory
Minds
Needs
Opportunity
Partner
Past
Pleasure
Power
Present
Problem-solving
Reflection
Research
School
Skills
Spectrum
Teaching
Understanding
Universe
Work

Adjectives

Accurate
Authoritative
Best
Broad
Caring
Changing
Comfortable
Committed
Comprehensive
Contemporary
Convenient
Cost-effective
Cultural
Current

Dedicated
Democratic
Distinct
Dynamic
Economical
Equal
Exciting
Expert
Fast
Economical
Essential
Excellent
Extensive
Efficient
Friendly
Great
Innovative
Inviting
Personal
Professional
Popular
Relevant
Responsive
Rewarding
Scholarly
Skilled
Superior
Timely
Useful
Varied
Vast
Vibrant
Vigorous
Vital
Welcoming

Inviting ideas is a good way to engage board members, staff, and others in thinking about the role of the library, what makes it unique, and what is most important. Whether this is done in writing or through dialogue, it is important that staff, board members, and top administrators have an opportunity to contribute. Opening up the process allows fresh insights and a sense of ownership to emerge.

But more heads aren't necessarily better when it comes to actual writing. After you have collected enough input, give the task of writing-editing to a staff member with a flair for words or a freelance writer. Be sure to allow enough time for writing, review, and revision. Three drafts should be enough to reach consensus, with the library director or board serving as final arbiter.

The following steps represent one approach to drafting a mission statement that is efficient and encourages buy-in from key groups. It assumes that one or two people will be assigned the task of writing and editing based on the input received.

1. Invite board members and staff to submit their suggestions for a mission statement. Provide criteria.
2. Establish a work group composed of representatives from key groups, such as the board and staff, as well as a writer-editor. Give them copies of suggestions received and relevant materials, such as the previous mission statement, comments from library users about the value of the library, brochures, or speeches.
3. Provide a facilitator or allow the group to select a discussion leader.
4. Adopt goals, criteria, and a timetable. Identify key audiences, style, and potential formats for the mission statement.
5. Brainstorm key concepts to be included in the statement.
6. Allow writer to draft a statement.
7. Submit the draft statement to the work group for comments.
8. Refine the statement based on feedback.
9. Submit a second draft for review.
10. Test the statement with people from outside the library. Does it have the desired effect?
11. Refine and prepare a third draft for key groups: board, staff, Friends.
12. Make final edits and present to the library board or parent group for approval.

Figure 3-2 suggests some useful questions to guide your group in drafting a mission statement.

FIGURE 3-2
Brainstorming

Try answering the following questions, individually or as a group, as a guide in drafting the mission statement.

- What three qualities or characteristics come to mind when you think about the library?
- Whom does the library aim to serve?
- What is its primary focus or contribution?
- Who needs to hear this message (internal and external audiences)?
- What makes the library unique? What benefits does it offer that no else does?
- Why is the library important—to individuals, your community, or a parent institution?
- How does it fulfill its mission?
- What kind of tone or personality should the library have?

A different approach

"The Daly City Public Library is committed to providing and promoting access to materials and services that meet the needs and interests of a diverse community in a professional, helpful manner." (1994)

"Preserving yesterday
Informing today
Inspiring tomorrow" (2002)

While most organizations take a group approach to drafting a mission statement, the Daly City Public Library's director, Susanna Gilden, now retired, took a different tack. "I'd been through processes where we did mission statements in a group and wordsmithed them to death and came up with something that nobody remembered," she explained.

When it came time to update Daly City's statement, Gilden says she sought her staff's input but none was volunteered. "I like to play with words, so I took that as license to do so."

She came up with the phrase at home on a Saturday afternoon. "It was an epiphany," she recalls. "It has all the words we do and say. The board loved it. When I announced it at our city department heads meeting, they all clapped.

Staff can say it without being embarrassed. And I can say it to the city council and they hold their heads up high."

Her advice to others: "Keep it short, punchy, and descriptive. If you have someone who's creative with words, send him or her off to do it."

Of her own effort, she says, "I self-edited a lot. It's the culmination of twenty-nine years of public librarianship. I probably couldn't have thought of it in year one."

In critiquing the library's previous mission statement, Gilden says, "It's OK. It's making a nod toward diversity, broad interests, and professionalism—all the things you want to say. But those things shouldn't have to be put in writing. How you deliver the service—and to whom you deliver it—should be understood. It's your community, and it is diverse. Those are givens."

MAKING A GOOD STATEMENT BETTER

In many cases, the difference between a good mission statement and a great one is simply a matter of editing and organization. Substituting active voice for passive, deleting unnecessary words, and replacing jargon with plain English may be all it takes to add punch. Some phrases may be more appropriate if included under goals, values, or strategies. A streamlined statement can be more vibrant and powerful without diluting your plan.

Following are examples of mission statements before and after editing. In each case, an effort was made to preserve the emphasis of the original while enlivening the language and keeping it under twenty-five words. Imagine seeing them framed and hung in the library.

Academic libraries

Before

> The mission of the —— Library lies in identifying, organizing, preserving, and making accessible the resources which are the basis for scholarly, vocational, and recreational inquiry and the exploration of new fields of study in support of the college curriculum and general enrichment. Through ongoing development of networked information resources and maintenance of comprehensive print-based collections, we will continue to provide relevant and innovative library services to students, faculty, staff, and the community.

After

> The mission of the —— Library is to educate, inform, and enrich students, faculty, staff, and the greater community.

Before

> The —— Library has established as its mission to make available to students, faculty, staff and community patrons resources and services that support and enrich the curricula and contribute to the intellectual and cultural development of the college community.

After

> The —— Library provides resources and expertise that support the intellectual and cultural development of faculty, staff, and community users.

Research libraries

Before

> The —— Library is a dynamic research environment that supports the curriculum and mission of the University. It provides

> - Collections, selected, organized and preserved to meet the curricular and research needs of the University community;
> - Access to quality print, media, and digital resources and appropriate information technology;
> - Quality services to assist users in fulfilling their information needs;
> - Instruction to enable the development of research skills and critical thinking;
> - An accessible place for study and research.

After

> The —— Library provides a dynamic research environment with extensive resources and staff to assist faculty, students, and others with their information needs.

Before

> The mission of the —— Library is to develop collections that support the educational and research programs of the University and to provide services for the benefit of university and research communities and the residents of the state of ——. The Library's mission is to support, participate in, and enhance the instructional, research, and public services activities of the University by placing priority on service to students, faculty, and staff; by acquiring, organizing, preserving, communicating, and sharing the record of human knowledge; and by teaching people how to use libraries effectively and access information successfully.

After

> The —— Library connects the academic and research communities and the people of —— with the record of human knowledge.

Public libraries

Before

> A basic municipal service, the —— Library provides current information, formal education support, independent learning opportunities and life enrichment materials to a highly diverse public in a warm and welcoming atmosphere through a highly trained team of individuals committed to quality service.

After

> We enrich lives with resources and opportunities for lifelong learning and enjoyment. Our expert staff is here to help with your information needs.

Before

> The —— Library provides materials and services of popular interest to the community, emphasiszing and encouraging reading by children, supplementing the educational needs of the community, and furnishing timely, accurate information.

After

> The ——— Library builds a community of readers with collections, services, and staff who encourage children and adults to read for learning and enjoyment.

School libraries

Before

> Our mission is to promote active learning by assisting students to access, evaluate, and utilize information. The library recognizes the importance of ethical behavior in a world increasingly independent on information technology.

After

> We prepare students for a lifetime of learning. We teach students to find, evaluate, and use information in a responsible manner.

Before

> The mission of the ——— School District Libraries is to support and enhance the teaching and learning environment and to promote recreational reading by providing comprehensive, multicultural collections that allow all students and faculty access to a wide variety of print and nonprint materials using current technology.

After

> The ——— School District Libraries provide resources and staff to help teachers teach and encourage students to read and learn about their world.

CHAPTER 4

Putting Your Statement to Work

Finding the right words to communicate your mission is a challenge. But writing your mission statement is not an end in itself. It is a beginning.

A well-defined mission statement makes planning easier by providing a clear focus for the library's activities. Along with your vision statement and values, it helps to define your work culture. It serves as a touchstone to guide you in making hard decisions about priorities as well as everyday judgment calls.

Presenting and discussing the finalized mission statement with staff, board members, and other key groups are essential if it is to become a living document. Everyone, including part-time and student employees, delivery drivers, and custodians, should understand the mission and how their responsibilities and duties relate to it. The mission statement should be a part of all orientation sessions and provide a focal point for ongoing discussions about library management and operations.

A mission statement that works as both a planning and a communication tool sends a powerful message. The Daytona Beach Community College Library posts its mission statement in both staff and public service areas. "I could say it in my sleep," says Yvonne Newcomb-Doty, dean, Business, Distance Learning & Library Services. "My guess is so could most of the staff. They know if they are not facilitating, sustaining, or encouraging they are not doing their job—they must be at lunch, on break, or goofing off. It's that simple."

Kim Grimes, teacher-librarian at Corbett Elementary School in Tucson, Arizona, puts it another way: "If you can't articulate the mission, how can you

BB

Films: on Demand.

effectively communicate the importance of school libraries? How can you work collaboratively with teachers if you—and they—don't understand your role?"

Handsomely framing and displaying your mission is a sign of pride and your openness to accountability. The Mead Public Library in Sheboygan, Wisconsin, posts a framed copy of its mission next to the elevator along with the names of the mayor, city council, and library board—an implicit invitation to let governing officials know how well the library is fulfilling its mission.

The Chicago Public Library's "Read, Learn, Discover" mission/slogan is built into the floors, walls, or facades of new branches. The message has been hung on street pole banners across the city and appears in brochures, on signs, and on staff business cards. Framed copies of the full-text mission statement appear on service desks.

The library continues to refine how it uses the statement and how it relates to other images, logos, and taglines. Former Marketing Director Jamey Lundblad, now director of communication strategies for a design communication firm, says, "Just as it's important to select which programs, services and initiatives to pursue based on your institution's mission, it's equally important to use the mission as a guide for which marketing programs to pursue and in deciding how the library should be portrayed."

The mission statement is central to how the library seeks to position itself in the minds of others. The statement or a short version of it should appear routinely in key publications—the annual report, brochures, employee handbook, and website communications. It should be a core part of presentations to funding bodies and community—and not just at budget time.

Another marketing strategy in which the mission statement can play a key role is word of mouth. Anyone who has read a book or gone to a movie recommended by a friend knows that word of mouth is the most powerful form of advertising. It is also the cheapest. But simply talking to people isn't enough. For word-of-mouth marketing to work, there must be a focused, consistent message that is easy to remember and say. With millions of enthusiastic users and supporters, libraries are ideally positioned to harness the power of their mission statements. Staff, trustees, and Friends will join in delivering the message.

A growing number of libraries are discovering the power of using their mission statement to make a public statement. Here's what some of them are doing:

- In California, the Daly City Public Library awarded pins with its new mission statement to staff, trustees, and city council members during National Library Week.
- The Hennepin County Library in Minnetonka, Minnesota, published *Strategic Directions 2001-2005,* a four-color brochure that highlights its

mission and vision statements, critical success factors, strategies, and priority action plans.

- The Lake Agassiz Regional Library in Moorhead, Minnesota, put its mission statement on coffee mugs and computers.
- The Public Library of Des Moines (Iowa) Foundation has its mission statement painted on the wall of its office.
- In Florida, the Orange County Library's statement appears on its library card and on chocolates and other giveaways.

Whether displayed on the library's home page or framed and hung on the wall, a well written, thoughtful mission statement provides an ongoing source of inspiration and guidance. Used strategically as part of an overall marketing plan, it is a first step toward having your library's services be understood and valued.

SPOTLIGHTING YOUR MISSION

A walk through your library or a look through a novelties catalog will suggest many ways to spotlight your mission statement. Possibilities include:

Bookbags	Pens
Bookmobile	Plaques
Business cards	Posters/bookmarks
Customer comment cards	Presentation folders
E-mail signature	Signs at circulation and service desks
Fans (handheld)	
Letterhead	Stained glass window
Newsletters for the public and staff	Tent cards (similar to those found in restaurants)
Paperweights	Window decals

CHAPTER 5

Mission Statements

The following mission statements are intended as a source of inspiration. Don't limit yourself to libraries of your own type, as there may be language or other elements to borrow. Most of these statements were written before one- or two-sentence statements became the rule. Not all of them meet all the criteria outlined in this book, but they meet some—whether it's brevity, good use of language, or a clear focus. Permission has been granted to publish these statements in this book. If you wish to borrow or adapt, contact the library or institution listed. If you have a mission statement or an idea for using it that you would like to share, please send it to librarycomm@librarycomm.com for posting on an updated on-line collection of mission statements.

The institutions included here are listed alphabetically within the following categories:

Academic Libraries

    College

    Community College

    University

Public Libraries

    Population under 50,000

    Population 50,000–99,999

Population 100,000–249,999
Population 250,000–499,999
Population over 500,000

Research Libraries
Archives/Special Collections
Independent
University

School Library Media Centers
Elementary
Middle School/Junior High
School District
High School

More Mission Statements
Associations
Boards of Trustees
Foundations
Friends of Libraries
Regional/State Libraries

ACADEMIC LIBRARIES

Colleges

Bethel College Library
3900 Bethel Drive
Saint Paul, MN 55112
(651) 638-6222
http://library.bethel.edu

MISSION STATEMENT

The mission of the BCL is to create a stimulating environment which will promote the quest of knowledge and encourage academic excellence. Resources, equipment and instruction will be continually updated and expanded to keep pace with constantly changing information and technology. The staff will facilitate access to resources of varied formats and locations and will be the catalyst that empowers students, faculty, and staff to grow intellectually and to work effectively within and beyond the Bethel community.

Laurence McKinley Gould Library
Carleton College
One N. College Street
Northfield, MN 55057-4097
(507) 646-4260
(507) 646-4087 Fax

MISSION STATEMENT

The Laurence McKinley Gould Library serves Carleton by collecting, preserving, and building connections to the record of human knowledge. By creating a setting conducive to learning, discovery, and cultural excitement, we help faculty, students, and staff meet academic and personal goals that extend knowledge and promote achievement in the individual and in the community.

Van Wylen Library
Hope College
53 Graves Place
P.O. Box 9012
Holland, MI 49422-9012
(616) 395-7790

MISSION STATEMENT

The mission of the library is to serve as a vibrant center of intellectual and cultural life at Hope College by assuming a significant educational role in a college community committed to excellence in learning and teaching.

The library will facilitate individual and collaborative learning and exploration by providing physical and virtual environments, and the technology and staff to support them.

The library will foster a community of information-literate, lifelong learners by coordinating and implementing a comprehensive instruction program designed to reach a variety of information needs and learning styles.

The library will collect, organize, and provide access to information sources that support the college's undergraduate liberal arts curriculum, and the intellectual, cultural, and spiritual growth of the Hope community.

Millard Sheets Library
Otis College of Art and Design
Ahmanson Building, Goldsmith Campus
9045 Lincoln Boulevard
Los Angeles, CA 90045
(310) 665-6930
http://www.otis.edu/library

MISSION STATEMENT

The Millard Sheets Library provides a learning environment designed to inspire creative students and faculty at Otis College of Art and Design.

Villa Maria College Library
204 Pine Ridge Road
Buffalo, NY 14225-3999
(716) 896-0700
http://villa.edu

MISSION STATEMENT
The mission of Villa Maria College Library is to provide resources and services that support the teaching mission of the college and to assist students in becoming information literate.

Community colleges

Andrew G. Truxal Library
Anne Arundel Community College
101 College Parkway
Arnold, MD 21012-1895
(410) 777-2211
http://www.aacc.cc.md.us/library/aacclib1.htm

MISSION STATEMENT
The Andrew G. Truxal Library is committed to participating in teaching and promoting lifelong learning at Anne Arundel Community College and throughout Anne Arundel County by:

- Providing services that foster student success and enrich student learning;
- Establishing and maintaining access to information resources that support the College's curriculum;
- Teaching information literacy skills that empower students to effectively find, use and evaluate information;
- Assisting in the assessment of student learning;
- Collaborating in a spirit of collegiality with faculty in the process of teaching and learning;
- Providing a source for intellectual, cultural and physical vitality in the community;
- Creating an environment that welcomes a diverse College and community population by critically evaluating the Library's collections, programs and services on a regular basis.

Carroll Community College Library and Media Center
1601 Washington Road
Westminster, MD 21157
(410) 386-8340
http://www.carroll.cc.md.us/library

MISSION STATEMENT

The Carroll Community College Library and Media Center seeks to empower its users by creating a learning environment conducive to the advancement of information literacy. The Library provides access to print, electronic, and audio-visual media to serve the information needs of the students, faculty, and staff of the College.

Daytona Beach Community College
1200 International Speedway Boulevard
Daytona Beach, FL 32114
(386) 254-3055
http://www.dbcc.cc.fl.us/library

MISSION STATEMENT

Our mission is to encourage, facilitate, and sustain learning in the DBCC community.

James Sprunt Community College Library
Boyette Building
P.O. Box 398
Kenansville, NC 28349-0398
(910) 296-2474
http://www.sprunt.com/library.html

MISSION STATEMENT

The James Sprunt Community College Library is responsible for developing and delivering learning resources, services, and programs which enrich and support the College curriculum and help students meet their educational goals.

Oakland Community College Libraries
739 S. Washington Avenue
Royal Oak, MI   49067
(248) 246-2525
http://www.occ.cc.mi.us/library

MISSION STATEMENT

The primary mission of the Oakland Community College Libraries is to provide information resources and services for students in support of the college curriculum, including instruction and guidance in the development of information literacy. The Libraries also provide for the general information needs of faculty, staff, and community patrons. To fulfill this mission, OCC Libraries strive for a balanced collection of sources in both traditional and electronic forms.

Walla Walla Community College Library
500 Tausick Way
Walla Walla, WA   99362
(509) 527-4294
http://sql.wwcc.edu/lib

MISSION STATEMENT

Walla Walla Community College Library provides instructional resources and services to students, faculty, staff, and community patrons. Its resources are appropriate to the curriculum in both format and content. Its collections are well organized and easily available; its technology is current; and its service is fast, courteous, and knowledgeable.

Universities

Howard University Libraries
500 Howard Place NW
Washington, DC 20059
(202) 806-7234

MISSION STATEMENT

Howard University Libraries is a forward-looking organization, dedicated to providing the highest standards in service and resources that support the University mission for excellence in learning, scholarship and service. In a society increasingly dependent on information technology and lifelong learning, we are committed to fostering information empowerment for academic and professional success, with a distinct commitment to preparing people of color and the economically disadvantaged for leadership and service to our nation and the global community.

Idaho State University Libraries
850 S. Ninth
P.O. Box 808
Pocatello, ID 83209-8089
(208) 236-2997
http://www.isu.edu/library

MISSION STATEMENT

The Idaho State University Libraries serve the University community by providing collections and services in support of the University's teaching and research missions. As the largest state-supported library in southeast Idaho, the Libraries also play a role in the development of University cooperative programs and in the provision of library services to the citizens of Idaho.

New Mexico State University Library
Dept. 3475
P.O. Box 30006
Las Cruces, NM 88003-8006
(505) 646-2932
http://lib.nmsu.edu

MISSION STATEMENT

The New Mexico State University Library develops and provides essential and specialized resources and services to the NMSU community and the people of New Mexico. The Library does this by:

- selecting, acquiring, and organizing resources;
- providing human and technologically mediated access;
- teaching users to locate, obtain, and evaluate information.

The Library provides leadership to New Mexico State University in:

- the distribution of scholarly information;
- collaborative information projects;
- electronic access and delivery of information.

Ohio Wesleyan University Libraries
LA Beeghly Library
43 Rowland
Delaware, OH 43015-4431
(740) 368-3225
http://library.owu.edu

MISSION STATEMENT

We, the staff of the Ohio Wesleyan University Libraries, support the teaching, study, and research activities of the University. We enthusiastically serve the community of scholars by acquiring, organizing, and preserving information, and by teaching its ethical and effective use. We actively encourage the lifelong pursuit of knowledge.

University of Texas at Arlington
P.O. Box 19497
Arlington, TX 76019
(817) 272-1413
http://www.uta.edu/library

MISSION STATEMENT

The UTA Libraries bring together knowledgeable staff, scholarly information, welcoming spaces, and leading-edge technology to promote learning and enable research. First and foremost we serve UTA students and faculty. We also serve as a valuable resource for University staff and for the community beyond the campus.

PUBLIC LIBRARIES

Under 50,000

Bettendorf Public Library Information Center
2950 Learning Campus Drive
Bettendorf, IA 52722
(563) 334-4175
(563) 344-4185 Fax
http://www.rbls.lib.il.us/bpl

MISSION STATEMENT

The Bettendorf Public Library Information Center is committed to providing access to information and ideas for all.

Camden Public Library
55 Main Street
Camden, ME 04843
(207) 236-3440
(207) 236-6673 Fax
http://www.camden.lib.me.us

MISSION STATEMENT

The Camden Public Library is a cultural and intellectual center for the community. It provides, at a reasonable cost and in a friendly atmosphere, universal access to knowledge and lifelong learning through print, electronic resources, cultural activities, programs, and services. The library collaborates with other community groups to meet the educational, informational, and recreational needs of the entire community.

Campbell County Public Library
2101 S. 4J Road
Gillette, WY 82718-5205
(307) 687-0009
http://www.ccpls.org

MISSION STATEMENT

Our mission is to provide diverse cultural opportunities for reading, learning, and entertainment to all citizens of our community. We lead the way to a universe of information with personal service and technology.

Lititz Public Library
651 Kissel Hill Road
Lititz, PA 17543
(717) 626-2255
http://www.lititzlibrary.org

MISSION STATEMENT

The mission of the Lititz Public Library is to provide materials, services, and programs for educational, recreational, and cultural enrichment to residents of Lititz Borough, Warwick Township, and Elizabeth Township.

Westlake Porter Public Library
27333 Center Ridge Road
Westlake, OH 44145
(440) 871-2600
http://www.westlakelibrary.org

MISSION STATEMENT

Westlake Porter Public Library's mission is to educate, empower, enlighten, and excite the public by providing accessibility to and instruction in an array of resources in multiple formats on-site, and by linking individuals with resources and agencies off-site, that meet their information needs.

50,000–99,999

Emily Fowler Central Library
Denton Public Library
502 Oakland Street
Denton, TX 76201
(940) 349-8260
http://www.dentonlibrary.com

MISSION STATEMENT

The Denton Public Library enriches and advances the community by providing quality materials and services of informational, educational, leisure, and cultural value.

Greenwich Library System
101 W. Putnam Avenue
Greenwich, CT 06830
(203) 622-7900
http://www.greenwichlibrary.org

MISSION STATEMENT

The mission of the Greenwich Library System is to provide free and convenient access to information and to promote a love of reading and research; the joy of lifelong learning; and engagement with the arts, sciences, and humanities.

Mead Public Library
710 N. Eighth Street
Sheboygan, WI 53081-4563
(920) 459-3400
http://www.sheboygan.lib.wi.us/index.html

MISSION STATEMENT

The Mead Public Library provides collections and services designed to meet the educational and recreational needs of City of Sheboygan residents regardless of their age or formal schooling. The Library is a community information and cultural center. It provides the means through which City of Sheboygan residents may have free access to the thinking on all sides of all ideas. It provides access in a range of formats to fine works of literature, other works in the arts and sciences, and works reflective of the popular culture.

Newton County Library
7116 Floyd Street NE
Covington, GA 30014
(770) 787-3231
http://www.newton.public.lib.ga.us

MISSION STATEMENT

The Newton County Library provides materials and services to help community residents from children to adults to meet their informational, educational, recreational, and cultural needs. Materials are purchased in a variety of formats to stimulate appreciation of reading and learning.

Palatine Public Library District
700 N. North Court
Palatine, IL 60067
(847) 358-5881
http://www.ppld.alibrary.com/faq.htm

MISSION STATEMENT

The mission of the Palatine Public Library District is to encourage lifelong learning and enrichment through the exploration of books and other media and to provide services and materials which will promote a well-informed and literate community.

100,000–249,999

Ann Arbor District Library
343 S. Fifth Avenue
Ann Arbor, MI 48104
(734) 327-4200
(734) 327-4200 Fax
http://www.aadl.org

MISSION STATEMENT

The Ann Arbor District Library provides open access to information, resources, and services that support and enrich the lives of the community it serves.

Daly City Public Library
40 Wembley Drive
Daly City, CA 94015-4399
(650) 991-8025
http://www.dalycitylibrary.org

MISSION STATEMENT

Preserving yesterday
Informing today
Inspiring tomorrow

Gary Public Library
230 W. Fifth Avenue
Gary, IN 46402-1270
(219) 886-2484
http://www.gary.lib.in.us

MISSION STATEMENT

The Gary Public Library will provide educational, cultural information, and recreational services and materials that reflect the community's changing needs and interests. It will also serve as a contact point to community, regional, and national resources.

Medina County District Library
210 S. Broadway
Medina, OH 44256
(330) 725-0588
http://www.medina.lib.oh.us

MISSION STATEMENT

The mission of the Medina County District Library is to enhance the quality of life in Medina County by providing the resources and services necessary to satisfy the evolving informational needs and recreational pursuits of the community.

North Las Vegas District Library
2300 Civic Center Drive
North Las Vegas, NV 89030
(702) 637-0270
(702) 649-2576 Fax
http://www.ci.north-las-vegas.nv.us/Departments/Library/Library.cfm

MISSION STATEMENT

Providing comprehensive, quality public library services, programs, and materials to the North Las Vegas community in an inviting atmosphere.

St. Louis Public Library
1301 Olive Street
St. Louis, MO 63103-2389
(314) 241-2288
http://www.slpl.lib.mo.us

MISSION STATEMENT

The St. Louis Public Library will provide learning resources and information services that support and improve individual, family, and community life.

250,000–499,999

Chesterfield County Public Library
9501 Lori Road
Chesterfield, VA 23832
(804) 751-4955
http://www.co.chesterfield.va.us/HumanServices/Libraries

MISSION STATEMENT

The mission of the Chesterfield County Public Library is to bring people and information together in a cost-effective manner so that citizens may enrich their own lives. The library encourages and fosters reading at all age levels, whether for recreation or information, supports education and lifelong learning, and helps the public obtain information.

Johnson County Library
P.O. Box 2933
Shawnee Mission, KS 66201-1333
(913) 495-2400
http://www.jocolibrary.org

MISSION STATEMENT

The Johnson County Library provides access to ideas, information, experiences, and materials that support and enrich people's lives.

Richland County Public Library
1431 Assembly Street
Columbia, SC 29201-3101
(803) 799-9084
http://www.richland.lib.sc.us/index.htm

MISSION STATEMENT
Meeting our citizens' needs for reading, learning, and information.

Santa Clara County Free Library
1095 N. Seventh Street
San Jose, CA 95112-4434
(408) 293-2326
http://www.santaclaracountylib.org

MISSION STATEMENT
The Santa Clara County Library is an open forum promoting knowledge, ideas, and cultural enrichment. The library provides free access to informational, educational, and recreational materials and services. In response to community needs, the library provides diverse resources on a wide variety of subjects and viewpoints and helps people use these resources.

Over 500,000

Chicago Public Library
400 S. State Street
Chicago, IL 60605
(312) 747-4999
http://www.chipublib

MISSION STATEMENT
We welcome and support all people in their enjoyment of reading and pursuit of lifelong learning. Working together, we strive to provide equal access to information, ideas and knowledge through books, programs and other resources. We believe in the freedom to read, to learn, to discover.

Denver Public Library
10 W. Fourteenth Avenue Parkway
Denver, CO 80204
(720) 865-1111
http://www.denver.lib.co.us

MISSION STATEMENT

The mission of the Denver Public Library is to help the people of our community to achieve their full potential.

Hennepin County Library
12601 Ridgedale Drive
Minnetonka, MN 55305
(952) 847-8500
http://www.hclib.org

MISSION STATEMENT

Hennepin County Library promotes full and equal access to information and ideas; the love of reading; the joy of learning; and engagement with the arts, sciences, and humanities.

Multnomah County Library
205 N.E. Russell Street
Portland, OR 97212-3796
(503) 988-5402
http://www.multcolib.org

MISSION STATEMENT

The Multnomah County Library serves the people of Multnomah County by providing books and other materials to meet their informational, educational, cultural, and recreational needs. Multnomah County Library upholds the principles of intellectual freedom and the public's right to know by providing people of all ages with access and guidance to information and collections that reflect all points of view.

Orange County Library System
101 E. Central Boulevard
Orlando, FL 32801
(497) 835-7323
http://www.ocls.lib.fl.us

MISSION STATEMENT
Information, Imagination, Inspiration

RESEARCH LIBRARIES

Archives/Special collections

Colorado River Indian Tribes Library/Archive
Route 1 Box 23-B
Parker, AZ 85344
(928) 669-9211
http://www.critlibrary.com

MISSION STATEMENT
The purpose of the Colorado River Indian Tribes Library/Archive is to promote intellectual freedom, and to inspire ideas to the community at large, and to enrich tribal life by preserving and documenting the Mohave, Chemehuevi, Navajo, and Hopi culture for future generations.

Archives of Women in Science and Engineering
Iowa State University
Special Collections Department
403 Parks Library
Ames, IA 50011-2140
(515) 294-6672
(515) 294-5525 Fax
http://www.lib.iastate.edu/spcl/wise/miss.html

MISSION STATEMENT

The Archives of Women in Science and Engineering seeks to preserve the historical heritage of American women in science and engineering. To do this, the Archives solicits, collects, arranges, and describes the personal papers of women scientists and engineers as well as the records of national and regional women's organizations in these fields.

The Archives will also serve as a local, regional, national, and international resource for information on women in science and engineering, with a particular emphasis on K–12 and college-level students.

The Ohio State University Archives
2700 Kenny Road
Columbus, OH 43210-1046
(614) 292-3271
(614) 688-4150 Fax
http://www.lib.ohio-state.edu/arvweb

MISSION STATEMENT

The mission of the Ohio State University Archives is to serve as the official memory of the University. The Archives identifies, preserves, and makes available the documentation of continuing and historical value to the University. In addition, the University Archives provides archival services for the Byrd Polar Research Center and the John Glenn Institute. The Archives consists of four divisions: Byrd Polar Research Center Archival Program; John Glenn Archives; University Manuscripts; and University Photo Archives.

School of Law Library
University of Baltimore
1415 Maryland Avenue
Baltimore, MD 21201
(410) 837-4584
http://law.ubalt.edu/lawlib

MISSION STATEMENT

The Law Library's mission is to provide users with the easiest access to the broadest possible array of legal information sources; support faculty in their teaching and research; educate students in the use of legal information sources; and inform the public of those sources and their use. The staff has a strong service orientation, and it serves the students and faculty of the School of Law, alumni, other members of the University community, members of the Bar, and the public.

Independent libraries

Folger Shakespeare Library
201 E. Capitol Street SE
Washington, DC 20003-1094
(202) 544-4600

MISSION STATEMENT

The mission of the Folger Library is to preserve and enhance its collections; to render the collections accessible to scholars for advanced research; and to advance understanding and appreciation of the Library and its collections through interpretive programs for the public.

The Historical Society of Pennsylvania
1300 Locust Street
Philadelphia, PA 19107
(215) 732-6200
http://www.hsp.org/general/about.html

MISSION STATEMENT

The Historical Society of Pennsylvania inspires and nurtures historical appreciation of the Commonwealth of Pennsylvania and its place in the nation's history.
Founded in 1824 and significantly augmented in 2002 by the Balch Institute for
Ethnic Studies, the Society is a collector and steward of the documentary record
and an historical educator and publisher. The Society's collections inform its
interpretive and educational programs, and these engage wide publics, adding
depth and dimension to understandings of our diverse pasts and each other.

Art Collections and Botanical Gardens
Huntington Library
1151 Oxford Road
San Marino, CA 91108
(626) 405-2100
http://www.huntington.org

MISSION STATEMENT

Building on Henry E. Huntington's legacy of renowned collections and botanical gardens that enrich the visitor, the Huntington today encourages research
and promotes education in the arts, humanities, and botanical sciences through
the growth and preservation of its collections, through the development and
support of a community of scholars, and through the display and interpretation
of its extraordinary resources to the public.

Library of Congress
101 Independence Avenue SE
Washington, DC 20540
(202) 707-5000
http://www.loc.gov

MISSION STATEMENT

The Library's mission is to make its resources available and useful to the Congress and the American people and to sustain and preserve a universal collection of knowledge and creativity for future generations.

National Agricultural Library
10301 Baltimore Avenue
Beltsville, MD 20705-2351
(301) 504-5755
http://www.nal.usda.gov

MISSION STATEMENT

The National Agricultural Library ensures and enhances access to agricultural information for a better quality of life.
    The National Agricultural Library:

- Serves as a National Library of the United States and as the Library of the U.S. Department of Agriculture.

- Acquires, organizes, manages, preserves, and provides access to information and provides quality stewardship of its unique collection.

- Assists, trains, and educates people based on assessment of their information needs.

- Provides leadership in information management.

- Maximizes access to information through collaborative efforts and utilization of technology.

- Enhances global cooperation through international exchange of information and the provision of services and technical assistance.

University libraries

Harold B. Lee Library
Brigham Young University
2066 HBLL
Provo, UT 84602
(801) 378-2905
http://www.lib.byu.edu/hbll

MISSION STATEMENT

The Harold B. Lee Library supports the academic and religious mission of Brigham Young University and its sponsor, the Church of Jesus Christ of Latter-day Saints. The library's mission is to acquire, organize, preserve, and provide access to collections of scholarly and related materials in all media; to assist patrons in finding and using information available at the University and elsewhere; and to encourage lifelong learning.

Cornell University Library
201 Olin Library
Cornell University
Ithaca, NY 14853-5301
(507) 255-3689
http://www.library.cornell.edu

MISSION STATEMENT

Cornell University Library enriches the intellectual life of the University by fostering information discovery and intellectual growth, nurturing creativity, and partnering in the development and dissemination of new knowledge. Cornell University is a research university that aims to serve society by educating responsible citizens and extending the frontiers of knowledge.

Perkins Library System
Duke University
Durham, NC 27708-0190
(919) 660-5870
http://lib.duke.edu

MISSION STATEMENT

In active support of Duke University's mission: we provide to the University and wider academic community a place for self-education and discovery; we promote scholarship and good citizenship through information literacy; we acquire, organize, preserve, and deliver information resources and assist users in their effective use; we create a great library for a great University.

William and Gayle Cook Music Library
Indiana University Bloomington Libraries
Simon Music Library and Recital Center
200 S. Jordan Avenue
Bloomington, IN 47405
(812) 855-2970
(812) 855-3843 Fax
http://www.music.indiana.edu/information/mission98.html

MISSION STATEMENT

To support and strengthen music and dance performance, teaching, learning, and research by providing the collections, services, and environments that lead to intellectual discovery and cultural growth.

Massachusetts Institute of Technology Libraries
Rm. 14S-216
Cambridge, MA 02139-4307
(617) 253-5651
http://libraries.mit.edu

MISSION STATEMENT

The MIT Libraries are creative partners in the research and learning process. We select, organize, present, and preserve information resources relevant to education and research at MIT. We sustain these world-class resources and provide quality services on behalf of the present and future research and scholarly community. We build intellectual connections among these resources and educate the MIT community in the effective use of information. We want to be the place people in the MIT community think of first when they need information.

North Carolina State University Libraries
North Carolina State University
Campus Box 7111
Raleigh, NC 27695-7111
http://www.lib.ncsu.edu

MISSION STATEMENT

The NCSU Libraries is the gateway to knowledge for the NC State University community and partners. We define the leading edge of information services and collections in support of the university's mission and to further knowledge in the world.

SCHOOL LIBRARY MEDIA CENTERS

Elementary schools

French Hill Elementary School
2051 Baldwin Road
Yorktown Heights, NY 10598
(914) 243-8090
http://frenchhill.yorktown.org/library/french%20hill%20library.htm

MISSION STATEMENT

The mission of the French Hill Library is twofold:

- Introduce children to the rich and diverse children's literature available to them, and provide a way for them to interact with it.
- Empower children to be effective lifelong users of information. It starts right here, at the French Hill Library!

McCrorey-Liston Elementary Library Media Center
1978 State Highway 215 S.
Blair, SC 29015
(803) 635-9490
http://www.myschoolonline.com/site/0,1876,45665-140806-48-4605,00.html

MISSION STATEMENT

The mission of the McCrorey-Liston Elementary Library Media Center is to ensure that every child has the opportunity to explore his world through a variety of books and resources. We strive to help all students become independent users of information and lifelong readers.

North Elementary Library Media Center
440 N. Tenth Street
Noblesville, IN 46060
(317) 773-0482
http://www.noblesvilleschools.org/nobln.nsf

MISSION STATEMENT

The mission of the North Elementary Media Center is to prepare students for lifelong learning, informed decision making, a love of reading, and the use of information technologies.

Roosevelt Elementary School Library Media Center
921 Ninth Street
Ames, IA 50010
(515) 239-3785
http://www.ames.k12.ia.us/schools/roosevelt/media/media.htm

MISSION STATEMENT

The mission of the Roosevelt Elementary Library Media Center Program is to support, encourage, and instruct all members of our school community in the knowledge and use of information skills and processes to meet their individual interests and needs. This includes having available a well-developed and current collection of materials in a pleasant and safe setting.

Groves Library and Media Center
Savannah Country Day School
824 Stillwood Drive
Savannah, GA 31419
(912) 925-8800
(912) 920-7800 Fax
http://199.250.191.10/lower/departments/lower_media.html

MISSION STATEMENT

It is the mission of the media center to create an environment that encourages intellectual stimulation, provides access to quality information, and offers enrichment to the school community it serves.

Spring Ridge Elementary Library Media Center
9051 Ridgefield Drive
Frederick, MD 21701
(240) 236-1515
http://www.myschoolonline.com/folder/0,1872,23747-45375-26-2463,00.html

MISSION STATEMENT

The mission of the school library media program is:

- to encourage lifelong reading for pleasure and as a source of information
- to assist staff and students in becoming effective users of information resources

Middle school/Junior high

Hanford Secondary School Library Media Center
450 Hanford Street
Richland, WA 99352
(509) 371-2600
http://revolution.3-cities.com/~ngraf

MISSION STATEMENT

To provide access to information and to encourage and develop a love for all literature.

Northeast Middle School Media Center
181 Coeur de Ville Drive
Creve Coeur, MO 63141
(314) 415-7100
(314) 415-7113 Fax
http://www.pkwy.k12.mo.us/northeast/library

MISSION STATEMENT

The Media Center strives to support the educational needs of the staff and students with appreciation for individual learning styles and ability levels.

Takoma Park Middle School
7611 Piney Branch Road
Silver Spring, MD 20910
(301) 650-6444
(301) 650-6430 Fax
http://www.mcps.k12.md.us/schools/takomaparkms/academics/mediacenter/
mediacenter.html

MISSION STATEMENT

The mission of the TPMS Media Center is to provide an information center for students and staff. Through the teaching of information literacy skills the Media Center program hopes to ensure that students will become lifelong learners, independent thinkers, and readers for pleasure and personal development.

Timberwood Middle School Library Media Center
18450 Timber Forest Drive
Humble, TX 77346
(281) 641-3806
http://tms.humble.k12.tx.us/library/source/library.html

MISSION STATEMENT

The Library Media Center, with its broad collection of print and nonprint media, makes vital contributions to the educational program of TMS. It is a place for serious study and research as well as recreational reading. Its use by all students and staff is encouraged and welcomed.

Wayland Middle School Library Media Center
201 Main Street
Wayland, MA 01778
(508) 655-6670
(508) 655-2548 Fax
http://www.wayland.k12.ma.us/middle_school/saber

MISSION STATEMENT

The mission of the Wayland Middle School Library Media Center is to provide current, highly reviewed, curriculum-related materials and a variety of free reading options for its students. The Center also contributes resources that support information in new, growing areas of knowledge. The Center strives to open up avenues of research to all of its students by providing opportunities for instruction in research skills, information literacy, and media competency, while offering flexible scheduling for full class, small group, or individual instruction.

West Middle School
109 East Garfield
Martinsville, IN 46151
(765) 342-6628
http://msdadmin.scican.net/wmslibrary

MISSION STATEMENT

It is the mission of the school library media program to provide the highest quality materials and service to support and enhance the curriculum as well as the learning needs and styles of all students. Programs that model best instructional practices will be developed in conjunction with classroom teachers to enhance the educational development of each student through the creation of curiosity, fostering a love of reading, giving experience in evaluating information sources, and allowing children and teachers to become effective seekers of information and proficient users of technology.

School district libraries

Beverly Public Schools Library/Media Program
20 Colon Street
Beverly, MA 01915
(978) 921-6100
(978) 922-6597 Fax
http://www.beverlyschools.org/programs/library.shtm

MISSION STATEMENT

The library media centers of the Beverly Public School System offer a wide variety of programs and services centered on reading and information literacy which:

- promote access to a variety of media, including print, non-print, and electronic formats;
- provide instruction in the location, evaluation and use of information;
- stimulate student interest in reading;
- support the curriculum of the schools.

School Media Program
Bloomington School District 271
1350 W. 105th Street
Bloomington, MN 55431-4126
(612) 591-5400
http://www.bloomington.k12.mn.us/distinfo/technology/media/media.html

MISSION STATEMENT

The mission of the district media and technology program is to provide an environment in which all individuals in Bloomington are empowered to become lifelong learners and effective users of information, ideas, and technology.

Library Media Center
Buckeye Valley Local Schools
679 Coover Road
Delaware, OH 43015
(740) 369-8735
(740) 363-7654 Fax
http://www.buckeyevalley.k12.oh.us/bvlib.htm

MISSION STATEMENT

The Buckeye Valley Library Media Centers are dedicated to effectively educating students to succeed in the information age. The Library Media Center provides a diverse collection of materials that assists both students and staff and enriches the curriculum.

Kansas Public Schools Library Media
625 Minnesota Avenue
Kansas City, KS 66101
(913) 279-2234
http:// www.kckpl.lib.ks.us/kckpl/index.html

MISSION STATEMENT

The mission of the library media center program is to provide the skills, experience and confidence that will enable students to use libraries and information resources for lifelong learning.

Rockwood School District
Mission 111 E. North Street
Eureka, MO 63025-1129
http://www.rockwood.k12.mo.us/library/default.htm

MISSION STATEMENT

The mission of the library media program is to provide a well-organized array of quality material that supports the curriculum, stimulates academic achievement, and encourages the development of lifelong learners.

Yuma School District One Library Media Services
450 Sixth Street
Yuma, AZ 85364
(928) 782-6581
http://www.yuma.org/library.html

MISSION STATEMENT

The mission of Library Media Services is to provide resources for instructional and recreational use by district students and teachers. These resources include publications, video and audio tapes, and electronic media. The resources support the teachers in enhancing the learning experience for the students and encourage the students to become lifelong learners.

High schools

Instructional Media Center
Hunterdon Central Regional High School
84 Route 31
Flemington, NJ 08822
(908) 782-5727
http://www.hcrhs.hunterdon.k12.nj.us/main.html

MISSION STATEMENT

The mission of the Hunterdon Central Regional High School Instructional Media Center (IMC) is to provide an engaging learning environment that establishes the foundations for lifelong learning and empowers the student to be an active participant in an information rich society.

Library Media Center
James River High School
3700 James River Road
Midlothian, VA 23113
(804) 378-2426
http://chesterfield.k12.va.us/Schools/James_River_HS/home.html

MISSION STATEMENT

Our mission is to meet the lifelong learning needs of our students and staff through a teaching partnership that integrates information literacy with the curriculum area standards of learning.

Lawrence High School Library
1901 Louisiana Street
Lawrence, KS 66046-2999
(785) 832-5050
http://library.lhs.usd497.org

MISSION STATEMENT

Lawrence High School
    Resources

    Education

    Adventure

    Diversity

    Success

At the Library!

Lufkin High School Library Media Center
309 S. Medford
Lufkin, TX 75904
(936) 630-4157
(936) 632-7831 Fax
http://www.lufkinisd.org/lhshome/library/lhsmain.htm

MISSION STATEMENT

The Lufkin High School Library Media Center enables students to develop a life-long love of reading and to acquire the essential skills of locating, evaluating, and using information for problem solving.

Monte Vista High School Library
3131 Stone Valley Road
Danville, CA 94526
(925) 552-2813
http://www.mvhs.net/~library

MISSION STATEMENT

Our mission is to support the curriculum of Monte Vista High School by providing access to materials that are relevant, appropriate, and current. We teach and promote information literacy and responsibility, and encourage reading for information and inspiration.

Traverse City Central High School Library
P.O. Box 32
1150 Milliken Drive
Traverse City, MI 49684
(231) 933-3640
http://www2.tcaps.k12.mi.us/csh/media/index.htm

MISSION STATEMENT

The mission of the Traverse City Central High School library media program is to ensure that students and staff are effective users of ideas and information. In support of that mission, our objective is to team with teachers to facilitate student learning.

MORE MISSION STATEMENTS

Associations

Alaska Association of School Librarians
http://www.akla.org/akasl/home.html

MISSION STATEMENT

To advance a high standard for the school librarian profession and the library information program in the schools of Alaska.

Hawaii Association of School Librarians
P. O. Box 235019
Honolulu, HI 96823
http://www.k12.hi.us/~hasl

MISSION STATEMENT

The mission of the Hawaii Association of School Librarians (HASL) is to advocate excellence, facilitate change, develop and provide leaders in the school library media field through collaborative efforts.

Friends of Kansas Libraries
Hutchinson Public Library
901 N. Main
Hutchinson, KS 67501
(316) 663-5441
http://skyways.lib.ks.us/KSL/fokl

MISSION STATEMENT

To encourage and support new and existing local Friends groups, to facilitate the exchange of useful information among organizations of Friends, and to advocate for excellent library services.

New York Library Association
252 Hudson Avenue
Albany, NY 12210-1802
(518) 432-6952
http://www.nyla.org/office/history.html

MISSION STATEMENT

The mission of the New York Library Association (NYLA) is to lead in the development, promotion and improvement of library and information services and the profession of librarianship in order to enhance learning, quality of life, and equal opportunity for all New Yorkers.

Ohio Library Council
35 E. Gay Street, Suite 305
Columbus, OH 43215
(614) 221-9057
(614) 221-6234 Fax
http://www.olc.org

MISSION STATEMENT

To serve as an advocate for public libraries and to provide opportunities for education and growth for library trustees, library Friends, library staff, and library-related personnel.

Boards of trustees

Fayetteville Public Library
217 E. Dickson
Fayetteville, AR 72701
(479) 442-2242
(479) 442-5723 Fax
http://www.fayettevillelibrary.org/board.htm

MISSION STATEMENT

The mission of the Board of Trustees is to provide leadership in performing the mission of the Library; serve as a liaison between the Library and City Council; and meet the informational, educational, and recreational needs of the community.

Harvard Public Library
Harvard Common
Harvard, MA 01451
(978) 456-4114
http://www.harvard.ma.us/librarytrustees.htm

MISSION STATEMENT

During their three-year, staggered terms, the six members of the Board of Library Trustees are charged with the task of governing the Harvard Public Library. They determine library policy, examine library needs and problems, and appoint the head librarian and other staff members. The Trustees are responsible for administering trust funds, approving expenditures of library funds, and presenting and recommending the library budget to the Finance Committee.

Tombstone Public Library
Fourth & Toughnut Streets
Tombstone, AZ 85638
(520) 457-3612
http://www.cityoftombstone.com/commissions.htm

MISSION STATEMENT

The Tombstone Library Board of Trustees is an advisory body to the Common Council regarding all matters of the Library including use, needs, and improvements.

Foundations

Foundation of Hennepin County Library
12601 Ridgedale Drive
Minnetonka, MN 55305
(952) 847-8634
http:// www.hclib.org/pub/info/support/foundation.cfm

MISSION STATEMENT

We seek to strengthen Hennepin County Library's value to the community.

- We pursue and secure funding and endowments.
- We fund special projects and services.
- We inspire community interest and involvement.

The Library Foundation, Inc.
Multnomah County Public Library
522 S.W. Fifth Avenue, Suite 1103
Portland, OR 97204
(503) 223-4008
(503) 223-4386 Fax
http://www.libraryfoundation.org

MISSION STATEMENT

To develop and encourage the private initiatives and gifts ensuring the people of Multnomah County the full measure of resources, services, and access befitting a great library.

Library of Michigan Foundation

702 W. Kalamazoo Street
P.O. Box 30159
Lansing, MI 48909
(517) 373-4470
http://www.michigan.gov/hal/0,1607,7-160-17445_19270_19410---,00.html

MISSION STATEMENT

The Library of Michigan Foundation secures funds for the Library of Michigan to strengthen and support the relevancy, availability, and accessibility of the Michigan libraries' resources and services for all Michigan residents.

Oakland Public Library Foundation

1611 Telegraph Avenue, Suite 801
Oakland, CA 94612
(510) 251-2466
(510) 251-2468 Fax
http://www.oplf.org

MISSION STATEMENT

The mission of the Oakland Public Library Foundation is to enhance the Oakland Public Library as a community resource by funding special projects and building an endowment for the support of the Library.

Public Library of Des Moines Foundation

100 Locust Street
Des Moines, IA 50309
(515) 283-4152
http://www.pldmfoundation.org/page.asp?pageid=2

MISSION STATEMENT

The mission of the Foundation is to raise funds and advocate for the public library system of Des Moines.

Friends of Libraries

Friends of Libraries and Archives of Texas, Inc.
P.O. Box 12516
Austin, TX 78711
(512) 463-5514
(512) 463-5436 Fax
http://castor.tsl.state.tx.us/friends

MISSION STATEMENT

The Friends' mission is to enrich library and archival services for the benefit of
the individual, the community, and the state by promoting and supporting the
programs of the Texas State Library and Archives Commission.

Friends of McAllen Memorial Library
601 N. Main
McAllen, TX 78501-4666
(956) 682-4531
(956) 682-1183 Fax
http://www.mcallen.lib.tx.us/friends.htm

MISSION STATEMENT

The mission of the Friends of the Library is to promote literacy, to support and
strengthen the McAllen Memorial Library Library and its branches, to provide a
means for the public to recycle their books and magazines, and to promote fel-
lowship among its members.

Friends of the Bethel College Library
3900 Bethel Drive
St. Paul, MN 55112
(651) 638-6065
http://library.bethel.edu/info/friends_library/index.asp

MISSION STATEMENT

The mission of the Friends of the Bethel College Library is to enhance the quality of the library collections, facilities, and services by encouraging gifts and estate
planning, awareness of library resources, and participation in library programs.

Friends of Fondren Library
Rice University
P.O. Box 1892
Houston, TX 77251-1892
(713) 348-5157

MISSION STATEMENT

The Friends of Fondren Library, founded in 1950, is dedicated to stimulating growth in library resources and facilities for the 21st century. The Friends seek to heighten community and alumni interest in Fondren Library and to support academic programs at Rice University by funding library collections and facilities.

Friends of Reed Library
SUNY College
Fredonia, NY 14063
(716) 673-3181
(716) 673-3185 Fax
http://www.fredonia.edu/library/friends.htm

MISSION STATEMENT

The mission of the Friends of Reed Library is to help promote a dynamic and mutually beneficial relationship between the college library, the community, and surrounding areas. The Friends also raise funds to assist in obtaining items to enhance the library's budget.

Regional/State libraries

Arkansas State Library
One Capitol Mall
Little Rock, AR 72201
(501) 682-1526
(501) 682-1899 Fax
http://www.asl.lib.ar.us/hours.html

MISSION STATEMENT

To provide the resources, services, and leadership necessary to meet the educational, informational, and cultural needs of the citizens of Arkansas, and to provide guidance and support for the development of local public libraries and library services.

Jefferson County Library Cooperative
2100 Park Place
Birmingham, AL 35203-2744
(205) 226-3615
(205) 226-3617 Fax
http://www.jclc.org

MISSION STATEMENT

The mission of the Jefferson County Library Cooperative is to foster, encourage, and enable cooperation among the public libraries of Jefferson County. We work together to provide the best public library services, information technology, and telecommunications in the world to the citizens of our county. We believe that our strength comes from our diversity, our unity of purpose, and our dedication to excellent service. By working with other institutions we further strengthen public library service and lifelong learning for all citizens of Jefferson County, Alabama.

Lake Agassiz Regional Library
118 S. Fifth Street
Moorhead, MN 56561-0900
(218) 233-3757
(218) 233-7556 Fax
http://www.larl.org

MISSION STATEMENT

The mission of Lake Agassiz Regional Library is to share resources in order to provide access to quality library services that meet lifelong learning needs and enrich the lives of those we serve.

South Carolina State Library
1430/1500 Senate Street
Raleigh, SC 29211
(803) 734-8660
http://www.state.sc.us/scsl

MISSION STATEMENT

The South Carolina State Library's mission is to improve library services throughout the state and to ensure all citizens access to libraries and information resources adequate to meet their needs. The State Library supports libraries in meeting the informational, educational, cultural, and recreational needs of the people of South Carolina.

Tri-State College Library Cooperative
Rosemont College Library
Rosemont, PA 19010
(610) 525-0796
(610) 525-1939 Fax
http://www.tclclibs.org

MISSION STATEMENT

The misson of the Tri-State College Library Cooperative is to advance, promote, and develop the best possible research and scholarship on the part of students and faculty members of participating colleges and research institutions and other persons interested in the educational process.

To these ends, the Cooperative shall facilitate the exchange of information among participants, encourage participants to share their library facilities, develop mutually supportive collection development/resource sharing programs, maintain and encourage communication and cooperation among the participants, and develop other mutually advantageous programs and activities.

Model Mission Statement— School Library Media Center

The model mission statement developed by the American Association of School Librarians, a division of the American Library Association, reads:

> The mission of the library media program is to ensure that students and staff are effective users of ideas and information. This mission is accomplished:
>
> - by providing intellectual and physical access to materials in all formats;
> - by providing instruction to foster competence and stimulate interest in reading, viewing, and using information and ideas;
> - by working with other educators to design learning strategies to meet the needs of individual students.

Written in 1988 as part of *Information Power: Guidelines for School Library Media Programs,* the statement is a timely and timeless definition of the role of the school library media center and its contribution. The statement and variations of it have been adopted by school library media centers across the United States. An excerpt, including the mission statement and goals, is available at http:// www.ala.org/aasl/ip_goals.html. Also see *A Planning Guide for Information Power: Building Partnerships for Learning* (Chicago: American Library Association, 1999).

APPENDIX B

Marketing Communication Plan Worksheet

Use this as a guide in developing a plan for your library.

(Name of Library)

1. *Introduction:* (Outline problems and opportunities to be addressed, relevant data, other background.)

   _____
   _____
   _____
   _____
   _____

2. *Communication goals:* (Describe the desired outcomes—big picture.)

   _____
   _____
   _____
   _____
   _____

3. *Objectives:* (Specify what you want to accomplish. These should be measurable and doable.)

   _____
   _____
   _____
   _____
   _____

4. *Positioning statement:* (How do you want people to think about the library? What should its image be?)

_____
_____
_____
_____
_____

5. *Key audiences:* (Who needs to hear the message?)
Internal: _____
_____
_____

External: _____
_____
_____

6. *Key message/Mission:* (List the most important thing you want people to know, plus three supporting points.)

_____
_____
_____
_____
_____

7. *Strategies:* (Outline publicity, promotion, and outreach activities. You will need to translate these into an action plan with a timetable and responsibilities.)

_____
_____
_____
_____
_____

8. *Evaluation measures:* (How will you know what worked and what didn't?)

_____
_____
_____
_____
_____

SUGGESTED READING

Abrahams, Jeffrey. *The Mission Statement Book: 301 Corporate Mission Statements from America's Top Companies.* Berkeley: Ten Speed Press, 1995.

American Association of School Librarians. *Information Power: Building Partnerships for Learning.* Chicago: American Library Association, 1998. Chapter 1 contains a model mission statement and goals for a school library media program. That information is also available at: http://www.ala.org/aasl/ip_goals.html. Accessed 4 April 2003.

———. *A Planning Guide for Information Power: Building Partnerships for Learning with School Library Media Program Assessment Rubric for the 21st Century.* Chicago: American Library Association, 1999.

Australian School Library Association. "School Library Mission Statements." Available at http://www.asla.nsw.edu.au/Libmissions.htm. Covers points to consider when drafting a mission statement; also includes sample mission statements from the U.S. and U.K. Accessed 4 April 2003.

Bettinger, Cass. "Strategic Planning That Computes." *Bank Marketing* 33, no. 8 (2001): 26–31. Directed at banks but a good general discussion of marketing strategy and how it relates to mission.

Brinckerhoff, Peter C. *Mission-Based Marketing.* New York: Wiley, 1997. A guide to the marketing process with the focus on how nonprofits can be both market-oriented and true to their mission.

DeCandido, GraceAnne. "Your Mission, Should You Choose to Accept It." *Wilson Library Bulletin* 69 (March 1995): 6. Discussion of what makes a good mission statement.

Feig, Barry. *Straight to the Heart.* New York: AMACOM, 1997. A look at strategic marketing with the emphasis on making an emotional connection and the mission statement as "the stepping stone to reaching the hearts and minds of customers."

Hartzell, Gary. "Controlling Your Own Destiny." *School Library Journal* 48, no. 11 (2002): 37. Clarifies the difference between mission and vision statements and explains why both are important.

Hastreiter, Jamie A., Marsha Cornelius, and David W. Henderson, eds. *Mission Statements for College Libraries.* 2d ed. Clip Notes, No. 28. Chicago: American Library Association, 1999.

Internet Nonprofit Center. "What Should Our Mission Statement Say?" Available at www.nonprofits.org/npofaq/03/21.html. A compendium of good advice. Accessed 4 April 2003.

Kassel, Amelida. "How to Write a Marketing Plan." *Marketing Library Services* 13, no. 5 (1999). A basic and sound guide to developing a marketing plan with the mission statement as starting point. Available at http://www.infotoday.com/mls/jun99/how-to.htm. Accessed 4 April 2003.

Knauft, E. B., Renee A. Berger, and Sandra T. Gray. *Profiles of Excellence: Achieving Success in the Nonprofit Sector.* A publication of Independent Sector. San Francisco: Jossey-Bass, 1991.

Leader to Leader Institute (formerly the Drucker Foundation). "How to Develop a Mission Statement." 1999. Step-by-step work plan for developing a mission statement. Available at http://leadertoleader.org/leaderbooks/sat/mission.html/. Accessed 4 April 2003.

Nelson, Sandra, for the Public Library Association. *The New Planning for Results: A Streamlined Approach.* Chicago: American Library Association, 2001.

Pathfinder Library System. "The Nuts and Bolts of Libraries." Available at http://www.colosys.net/pathfinder. Click on Mission Statements and Policies for a sampling of mission statements from public, school, and academic libraries in North America. Accessed 4 April 2003.

Steckel, Richard, and Jennifer Lehman. *In Search of America's Best Nonprofits.* San Francisco: Jossey-Bass, 1997.

INDEX